Cumbrian Brothers

Letters from Percy Kelly
to Norman Nicholson

David A. Cross

Fell Foot Press

Published by:
Fell Foot Press,
10, Red Gables,
Chatsworth Square,
Carlisle,
Cumbria, CA1 1HE,
England.
01228-525964

Distributed by:
Green Road Enterprises,
16, Green Road,
Kendal,
Cumbria,
LA9 4QR,
England.
01539-726134

British Library Cataloguing-in-Publication data:

Cross, David A.
Cumbrian Brothers: Letters from Percy Kelly to Norman Nicholson
1. Kelly, Percy, 1918-1993   2. Nicholson, Norman 1914-1987
3. Painting, Modern - twentieth century - England   4. Poetry, English

The introduction and edited text © David A. Cross 2007

The letters and pictures © The Estate of Percy Kelly are reproduced by courtesy of Maggie Sale and Rob David. Three further original letters, as indicated in the endnotes, are reproduced by courtesy of The University Librarian and Director, The John Rylands Library, The University of Manchester.

Percy Kelly's *Whitehaven from above St James's Church* and his print *Crane II, Hodbarrow Mine* are reproduced by courtesy of Abbot Hall Art Gallery, Kendal, Cumbria. His *Parton and Lowca Tip, Pica near Distington, Breton Cottages, Back Brow Methodist Church, Maryport* and *Fishing Boat CA 56* are reproduced by courtesy of a private collector and his drawing *Steam Engine, "Charlie"* is reproduced by courtesy of Katharine Whitehorn.

Norman Nicholson's photograph is reproduced by courtesy of Cressida Pemberton-Pigott.

ISBN   978-0-9553208-1-1

Designed and Printed by Reeds Printers Ltd., Penrith, Cumbria.

Acknowledgements

The author gratefully acknowledges the assistance of Rob David, Maggie and Julian Sale and Cressida Pemberton-Pigott with the photography; also Audrey Park, Christine Mills, John and Irene Kelly, Doreen Cornthwaite, Neil Curry, Sue David, Mary Burkett, Val Rickerby, Chris Wadsworth, Molly Lefebure, Allen Freer, Peggy Troll and the Norman Nicholson Society, Stella Halkyard of the John Rylands Library, Manchester University, the speakers at the Norman Nicholson conference organised by the Centre for North West Regional Studies in 2007, Hannah Neale, Sydney Chapman, Jackie Fay, Stephen White, Rachael Rodway, Dorathy Morgan, Pat O'Grady, Nicola Godfrey-Evans, the staff at Reeds Printers especially Simon Marston and to all others who have assisted in this project.

The publisher thanks the copyright holders for their permission to reproduce their material and would be glad to hear from the holder of one photographic copyright for whom he has sought in vain.

In memory of a dear friend, Joan David

Foreword

Shortly before her death in 2000, Joan David, the correspondent and friend of Percy Kelly, acquired a collection of Kelly's letters written to Norman Nicholson from 1971 to 1987. A further three letters from the collection had been deposited in the John Rylands Library at Manchester University (NCNI/1/158/1-3), and have been included in this book. None of these letters has previously been published, despite the current interest in both Percy Kelly and Norman Nicholson.

Unfortunately Norman Nicholson's replies have not survived, but Percy Kelly's letters on their own provide a rich insight into the thoughts of two 'Cumbrian Brothers', both leaders in their respective art forms.

Letter writing is a means of communication that has almost disappeared. For both Norman Nicholson and Percy Kelly it was an important means of keeping in touch when opportunities to meet face to face were infrequent. Towards the end of his life Norman Nicholson commented: 'I wrote an awful lot of letters - one kept in touch by correspondence.' Percy Kelly also maintained a voluminous correspondence until shortly before his death in 1993.

David Cross was a long time friend of Joan David and is the biographer of the eighteenth century Cumbrian artist George Romney. In 1976 he gave a course on Norman Nicholson's poetry for the British Council in Poland. He kindly agreed to write the introduction and to make the selections from the illustrated letters for this book.

Rob David, Kendal   July 2007

Norman Nicholson in conversation with David Wright, in P.N. Review, 46, Vol. 12, No. 2, 1985, pp. 41-44; Mary E. Burkett and Valerie M. Rickerby, Percy Kelly: A Cumbrian Artist, Skiddaw Press, 1997; Chris Wadsworth, The Painted Letters of Percy Kelly sent to Joan David 1983-1993, Castlegate House, 2004; Neil Curry (ed.), Norman Nicholson: Collected Poems, Faber, 1994; The Norman Nicholson Conference (2007) was organised by the Centre for North West Regional Studies on June 13th 2007.

Introduction

Unlike the creative spirits of the metropolis, many poets and artists of the Lake Counties have led their lives in relative isolation. Norman Nicholson (1914-1987), the poet of Millom, lived all his life in the remote south west corner of Cumberland and Percy Kelly (1918-1993), the artist from Workington, lived his latter years in St David's in Pembrokeshire and in rural Norfolk. They both sustained their friendships via a voluminous correspondence which, in Stella Halkyard's phrase at the Nicholson conference on June 13th 2007, 'transcended absence'. Nicholson corresponded with T.S. Eliot at Faber and Faber and with numerous other poets including Ted Hughes and Philip Larkin. Kelly mostly wrote to sympathetic collectors and curators. In their final years, correspondence became a lifeline for both men. The passages in this small volume are taken from letters written by Kelly to Nicholson between 1971 and 1987 and it is remarkable how many themes they had in common both in their correspondence and in their creative work.

In 1955 Percy Kelly met Norman Nicholson through an introduction from Allen Freer, an artist and inspector of schools in Manchester. Kelly was a thirty-seven year old postmaster of Great Broughton near Cockermouth while Nicholson, at forty-one, had already made his mark through the publication of *Five Rivers* in 1944. They corresponded, probably sporadically, from this date but the earlier letters have not yet come to light. As they were both from West Cumberland, Kelly empathised with the poet's mission to 'draw attention to things not usually thought of as part of the Lake District', in the words of Grevel Lindop at the Nicholson conference. The artist was already delineating the industrial environment and soon was to receive national plaudits himself.

Crane I, Hodbarrow Mine

Nicholson and Kelly were both deeply rooted in their native county and were from similar social backgrounds in coastal industrial towns. Both families, directly or indirectly, owed their living to the mining of coal and the production of steel and largely 'thrived on their iron diet', as Nicholson put it. They knew the dangers of the work; one of Nicholson's uncles had been killed in an iron-ore pit and Kelly's brother-in-law Henry Brennan had driven consignments of explosives to the mines. Also they both rejoiced in the contrasts between the grim urban terrain and the softer rural panorama and strove to create authentic representations of their locality in their different media. The poet's grandmother's house had a back street 'blocked by crags of slag', while the artist remembered how the noise of machinery was audible inside his grandparents' house in Maryport. For both, the Lake District fells were accessible and numerous summits feature in the work of both artist and poet. The Kellys attended the Primitive Methodist church and Nicholson's step-mother played the organ for the Wesleyan Methodists. However, although the poet's verse is steeped in his religious belief, such themes are not prominent in the artist's work. He did draw churches but his interest was architectural rather than spiritual.

Admirers of Kelly's work will already be familiar with the extraordinary spate of illustrated letters he sent to Joan David (1920-2000) between 1983 and his death in 1993. Other friends, curators, patrons and even buyers of individual works, including Nicholson, were the lucky recipients of the pages of his astonishing output and many of the finer examples are now framed and admired all over the country in private collections. Considering his anxious tendency to withold his full-scale artwork, his profligacy with the letters is quite remarkable. This can be explained by the fact that most of the illustrations are only small-scale copies of works which he retained in his own collection. They represent part of the total record of his creative achievement which he was convinced was of unique importance and which he was at pains to share with chosen correspondents. Indeed, as he wrote to Joan David, 'a thousand sketches, each part of the whole, [are] all held together by a fragile thread'. In addition, Kelly was conscious of the significance of his correspondence which he believed would gain him fame and he hoped that Mike Goldmark of the Goldmark Gallery in Uppingham, one of the dealers who pursued him, would write a book about him. The letters are full of biographical material which he intended to be read as a source 'for posterity'. Nicholson, in contrast, actually completed the autobiography, *Wednesday Early Closing*, as a record of his early life and many other details survive in his published verse and his own correspondence. Unfortunately his letters written to Kelly have not come to light. It is also a pity that the poet did not produce a second volume of autobiography.

Many artists sense the poetic element in their work and Kelly was no exception, claiming in a letter to Nicholson that 'the true artist whether figurative or abstract has to be part poet', and in another to Joan David 'it is my belief that without the poetic quality, fell paintings become very tedious, assuming the quality of a bad poem'. While in search of aesthetic uplift on the fells, he would write poems 'in my mind'. Kelly regularly read poetry and owned several volumes of Nicholson's work. He particularly refers in these letters to his copy of *Rock Face* (1948), to his enjoyment of *Weeds* and to painting a Millom composition to be framed together with one of Nicholson's poems, probably *On the Dismantling of Millom's Ironworks*. Nicholson also owned Kelly paintings of Maryport and Dockray. Other poets are quoted in the letters including Wordsworth,

John Clare and R.S. Thomas. Nicholson reciprocated with admiration and in *From Walney Island* used the artistic notion of the eye 'playing at poet with a box of colours'. Like many poets, notably Wordsworth, Kelly experienced moments when he had a powerful sense of his creative impulse. On one occasion he lay down prostrated in a barley field and on another occasion fell into an aesthetic trance while he was supposed to be playing a football match. Conscious of his own 'intense gift', he would have benefited from mentors but was reluctant to take advice. Nicholson not only had a more stable sense of his own creativity but was also more fortunate in his mentors.

As a popular performer, Nicholson read his verse with panache while Kelly was a 'great raconteur', always conscious of his audience and his ability 'to give pleasure' to the recipients of his letters. The artist was paradoxically very reluctant for much of his life to part with his paintings. Indeed, a whole caravanserai of dealers and collectors trekked north to woo him in largely fruitless attempts to buy work or to set up exhibitions. This flurry was in no small measure the result of Nicholson's friendship and encouragement and in one of the present letters, Kelly reproaches the poet writing: 'see what you have started'. Nicholson must have been somewhat frustrated when his friend sent them away empty-handed. Even Nicholson's niece, Liz Eastwick, who had generously subsidised Kelly's Norfolk fuel bills was dealt an ungracious refusal. Kelly was, in general, more likely to sell to friends or individuals than to representatives of the trade and his second wife Christine believes that this resulted from his need to be in control and from some sense that many works were unfinished. His twin brother John adds that the artist believed that 'the next painting would always be better'. Periodically, Kelly became quite excited by the prospect of a sale and he did agree to sell to major patrons such as the arts minister, Lord Eccles; the silk manufacturer, Sir Nicholas Sekers and Peter Scott, the chairman of the Provincial Insurance Company. Nicholson, on the other hand, was more straightforward in his dealings with both readers and publishers.

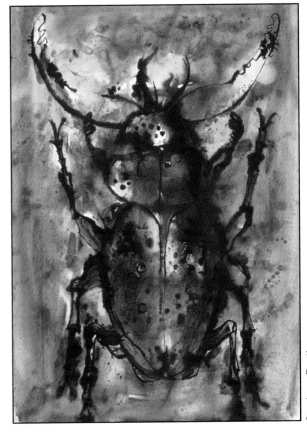

Staghorn Beetle

Kelly, as a demanding and self-absorbed correspondent, almost always devoted more time in his correspondence to his own affairs than to responding to the recipient's interests. His expectation that his correspondents would respond rapidly after he had done them the honour of a letter led to the collapse of several friendships. In the Joan David letters he expresses his frustration that Nicholson would often send him a brief postcard, rather than a proper letter. In July 1985, he even added that he is thinking of stopping writing to Nicholson, though it is not clear why he said this. Regrettably, now more immersed in his own troubles, he seems to have done so and no more letters between then and the poet's death in 1987 have yet come to light.

They were both, in different ways, auto-didacts. Kelly left school at fourteen and although Nicholson aspired to attend university, his health prevented this. Having spent many years reading widely, Nicholson tended to wear his learning lightly; whereas Kelly, when engaging with well-educated people, was at pains to demonstrate his intellectual ability by using French expressions, by making somewhat heavy-handed references to Cicero, Rousseau or Nietsche, or by quoting poetry. Kelly went to Art College very belatedly and is often rather ambivalent about the experience. Nonetheless, his ability to assimilate new ideas made him a good and wide-ranging conversationalist who regularly engaged in heartfelt discussions with strangers and who refers frequently to people enjoying these encounters. The poet, too, was sociable and happy talking to strangers, as he frequently did following his readings. Nicholson, having suffered from TB in childhood, had weakened lungs for the rest of his life, but made light of his debility. Kelly was physically more robust, but manifested hypochondria and depression, a gloomy side which is reflected in his 'dark drawings'. In his latter years he genuinely suffered from the dampness of Wales, poor eyesight and from tinnitus. At the end of their lives, both Nicholson and Kelly had serious problems with their throats: Nicholson's TB recurred and Kelly developed throat cancer.

Both men were conscious of the privilege of their creative lives and Kelly asserts his solidarity with Nicholson at several points. In discussing the creativity of art and poetry, Kelly insists on the importance of 'love, affection, integrity and humility' and praises Nicholson stating that as his work is born of these virtues, it 'stands out' from the rest. Nicholson was modest in his description of his own work, whereas Kelly tended to trumpet his successes, writing on occasion that he was about to produce 'a masterpiece'. Indeed, he was more capable of criticising others, both poets and artists, grumbling to Nicholson about 'poetry readings of a dubious type' and 'rotten poetry on the wireless'. He also disparages the Lake District artists who merely 'skim the surface' of their subject and exhibit work where 'the elusive indefineable quality' of the true artist never shows. Late in life he ends one letter with the pessimistic statement to Nicholson that 'we are a dying breed and there will be none to follow'. Happily, Nicholson was more optimistic.

Nicholson's writing encompassed numerous places in Cumbria but coastal industrial towns appear in many of his poems, from Barrow in the south to Whitehaven in the north. Kelly's coastal forays expressed themselves in representations of a wider range of places from Barrow to the Solway, but the two men held much in common. They had both travelled on the train which links the communities of the west coast and was captured by Nicholson as it 'canters along the curving shore'. The poet was very knowledgeable about the local geology of slate, sandstone and in particular the iron rich limestone of Hodbarrow Point as described in *Seven Rocks V* where 'steel nebs bore down to the hoard of ore.' Kelly in contrast, being more interested in technology, was fascinated by vintage cars, steam engines and their potent action; they both wrote of industrial cranes. However, the artist could not escape the ubiquity of the red haematite pigment of the iron in the soil and refers to his choice of this colour, in particular when describing his large work *Hodbarrow* which is now entitled *Millom, Cumberland* (Abbot Hall Art Gallery). Nicholson describes the ore as 'red as rhubarb' in *Five Rivers,* then notes in *The Blackberry* how red haematite dust even settles upon the fruit.

The poet and the artist also shared several interests, in particular a poignant sense of the decline of the range of mining and steelmaking processes which sustained their native communities. Neil Curry, the editor of *Collected Poems,* speaks of Nicholson's sense of the actuality and the harsh detail of this environment. Such toughness is ubiquitous in Kelly's own drawings and paintings of docks, industrial buildings and machinery which feature chimneys, cranes, working vessels, and the other lesser elements of the industrial landscape. Many of these feature in Nicholson's verse such as 'wheeled bogies', a 'lobster-armed crane' and the bastions of the colliery 'battlemented like a fort' in *Whitehaven* which for Kelly, probably reminded him of the profile of the Annie pithead at Workington (see front cover).

Indeed, after 1945, they both observed and recorded in pigment or in words, the dispiriting 'cold wind' of the inexorable sequence of closure, asset-stripping, vandalism and demolition of many of the key landmarks, not only of their own communities but also the neighbouring towns of Maryport, Whitehaven and to a lesser extent Barrow. Kelly observed that 'virtually the whole of West Cumberland closed down' and reminded his correspondent that there had even been steelworks at Cleator Moor, Distington and Harrington. They were left to observe the melancholy remains. Intriguingly, Nicholson uses agricultural metaphors to communicate these events such as 'the slagbanks ploughed down' and 'the chimneys felled'. The artist remembered 'the noise and light of the steelworks during the night' while this was soon followed by what the poet called the 'roar of its silence': the grievous loss of the familiar sounds of industry. Major phases of the decline are described in two of Nicholson's key verses: *On the Closing of Millom Ironworks* and *On the Dismantling of Millom Ironworks.* In a letter to Joan David, Kelly bewails how urban features sometimes seemed to disappear 'overnight' and reports the destruction of familiar machinery, in particular 'the beam engine at Hodbarrow'. Kelly also noted that Maryport 'was almost complete up to the 60s' but is now 'terribly scarred'. Kelly's brother-in-law Henry Brennan recalled that at one time there were as many as one hundred and sixteen belching chimneys between Maryport and Distington, but that not one now remains. In 1968, a symbolic coffin was carried throught the streets of Millom, a defiant gesture made by the workforce and a counterpart to the elegiac works of art made by these two creative friends. In *Wednesday Early Closing* (1975), Nicholson makes the radical suggestion that the National Trust should purchase an industrial landscape. Since that date, the Trust has acquired lead and graphite mines in central Cumbria, a recognition of the importance of industry in the landscape, but the sites of West Cumberland are still unrepresented.

Though the artist felt fortunate to have so many early drawings 'executed before the all-out demolition began', he regretted that he had not painted more as a 'record of departing and disappearing aspect[s] of life' in his earlier years. He was 'sure many of the studies [would] have historical interest in years to come'. In this response he is following the instinct of Ruskin who frequently drew buildings in Italy which he loved but knew would not be there when he next returned. Kelly recorded many landmarks and many 'priceless' buildings of the townscape which were lost in the 1960s when there was a 'mania to destroy anything old' and added how 'at the time it was as if my world was vanishing bit by bit'. Struck by the unusual design of Back Brow Methodist church in Maryport, he drew several elevations, showing its squat hexagonal steeple rising from the crossing. This church was later torched by vandals and Kelly observes how Christchurch by the harbour was left standing 'as if it were man's epitaph to a forgotten faith'. Mary Burkett rightly enthuses about these 'rare topographical records' of landmarks identified by the artist while at the Nicholson conference in 2007, David Cooper described how the poet, in a similar process, 'mapped out the environment' in his work.

Nicholson's verse periodically reflects his interest in vernacular architecture and includes references to 'slate bosses', 'Kirkby roundhead' slates and 'Coniston flagstones'. Kelly sees 'an almost human quality' in buildings, comparing the design and materials of the cottages of Pembrokeshire and Norfolk with those of Cumberland for the poet's benefit. He also cites John Betjeman's disparagement of the insensitive building of bungalows by 'settlers' and the inappropriate restoration of old cottages such as his favourite one in Loweswater now 'unrecogniseable having been tarted up'. Nicholson, according to Ian Brodie at the 2007 conference, shared this concern and hated the growing excesses of sterile tidiness in the countryside, imposed by urban off-comers. Isolated buildings which Kelly had observed carefully all his life were, of course, the central features of countless paintings. He particularly loved remote quirky terraces of houses such as Trumpet Terrace, Cleator Moor and Pica, near Distington (See p.40 and p.36).

Back Brow Methodist Church, Maryport

Knowing the west coast as well as they did, the artist and the poet also celebrate in their art the strange aesthetic of dereliction, Nicholson describing in *Provincial Pleasures* the beauty of the pit heads which display 'an elegance which is almost affected'. They both responded to the element of decay arising in the pit heaps of Nicholson's *Egremont* and in Kelly's tips and slag banks. This enthusiasm is also manifest in the artist's energetic scavenging from dumps and quarries. He salvaged a table from near Top Withens, the farm that inspired *Wuthering Heights*; removed other furniture from bonfire

Breton Cottages

piles and gathered materials for his Gospel Lane Gallery among rejected items from nearby R.A.F. Brandy. Most objects were functional but those from the beach, such as driftwood and water-worn glass, were arranged on windowsills at Glen Cottage.

Having been brought up on the coast, Kelly had great affection for boats and an image in his mind from childhood was of 'the forest of ships' masts in Senhouse Dock' at Maryport. He also recalled watching the 'steam cranes unloading tramp steamers with chipped black hulls, raw sienna painted superstructure, red oxide decks and tall smokestacks of innumerable colours'. In Cornwall and Brittany he captured small fishing boats, safe within the arms of the little harbours. Even when in London, a place he disliked, Kelly gravitated to the Thames and drew barges or tugs.

Kelly could be emotional in describing his empathy and kinship with the workers he encountered, perhaps from a sense of his descent from skilled craftsmen and his friendships with men made redundant during the period of industrial decline. Like Nicholson, he has 'enormous respect

for miners and steelworkers and dalesmen', the 'old characters who frequent the beach at Parton' and the folk he encounters in the villages of Norfolk who 'still retain old-fashioned virtues'. Despite this declaration, none of the artist's significant works include human figures or animals but, as he said to Molly Lefebure, the people were still there in his imagination, building fellside walls and mining beneath the ground. Similarly, Nicholson's verse in his early career does not feature individuals either.

Dream Boat

Nicholson professes in *Weeds*, not to like cultivated flowers and perversely empathises with species 'barred from the garden'. Kelly also preferred wild species, mourned their ephemerality and employed the bone-dry filigree of cow's parsley as a strengthening motif in paintings such as *Pica*. These attractive and delicate forms provided a powerful counterpoint to the ugliness and the potency of the industrial scene. Nicholson modestly suggested that he learned the names from cigarette cards but makes many references to specific and sometimes rare species such as ploughman's spikenard and sea spleenwort and uses a botanist's vocabulary such as calyx and corolla. For both men, each discovery of flowering plants on the edge of a slag heap was a precious moment, as the poet records in *Bee Orchid at Hodbarrow* and as the artist enthuses on finding columbine and honeysuckle on a 'scrap dump'. Apart from Nicholson's *Pot Geranium*, he celebrates numerous other species such as *The Bloody Cranesbill* and *The Grass of Parnassus*. Norfolk poppies, which bring much joy, appear widely in Kelly's work and he claims to prefer them to the wild flowers of Pembrokeshire. Both wild and cultivated species bloom on these pages including the harebell, white deadnettle, mimulus and sunflower. Extraordinarily, they both describe the joy of cupping a flower in the hand to appreciate the beauty, colour and form. At his mother's funeral, John Kelly recalls how his twin brother shocked the other mourners by arriving with an armful of the wild flowers she loved. At Nicholson's own funeral, his cousin Doreen Cornthwaite took wild flowers from Whicham, as Joan David took foxgloves to Kelly's.

Nicholson's rambles along the shore at Haverigg familiarised him with the many seabirds of the estuary which appear in his verse such as *The Black Guillemot*, while in *Whitehaven* 'curlews wheel on the north wind'. Kelly frequently drew birds including parrots, oyster catchers, lapwings and robins and kept at least two budgerigars. In one letter he records how the sound of the woodpeckers echoed from the sides of Melbreak and in another poetically captures a 'chirpy' little wren as 'a tiny miracle of feathers'. Nicholson wrote a poem *The Raven,* whilst one of Kelly's forbidding black and white prints featured the same bird flailing its wings. The artist spoke for both men when he wrote: 'I have always loved birds, flowers and bees'.

Pepi, his Budgerigar

That the two friends also shared a sense of humour is evident in Kelly's liking for Nicholson's poem *Weeds* and his comment to the poet in a letter in this collection that his own T.V. broadcast was re-scheduled to accommodate a dog show. Irvine Hunt acknowledges that Nicholson's humour was a major part of his appeal and some of his titles have a comic impact such as *Boo to a Goose*. In Wales, where Kelly struggled to maintain good relationships with his neighbours, he observed that the best way to travel was 'by broomstick'.

Both artist and poet held in their shared acquaintance a range of notable local figures, some of whom appear in the body of this text. Nicholson corresponded with Benjamin Britten and with numerous poets, several of whom are mentioned above, whilst Kelly maintained the signals equipment for Winston Churchill in his bunker at Hendon during the war and discussed art with this famous amateur painter. Indeed, they both had contact with royalty too: Kelly when King George VI viewed his paintings during an H.M. Forces exhibition at the National Gallery and Nicholson, accompanied by John Betjeman, when he collected the Queen's Medal for Poetry from Elizabeth II. That they were both taken seriously by such a range of prominent people is a further mark of their significance to posterity.

Helen Sutherland, an heiress, a collector and friend of Jim Ede of Kettle's Yard, invited many outstanding creative people including the artists Winifred and Ben Nicholson and the poets Elizabeth Jennings and Kathleen Raine, to her house Cockley Moor, at Dockray near Ullswater. Here she was, as Stella Halkyard observes, 'the hub of a kind of community with shared aesthetic and

Barn at Cockley Moor

literary interests'. Following his own visits, Nicholson wrote a poem *Cockley Moor* and in 1960 he kindly introduced her by letter to Kelly. Travelling by scooter for lunch, the artist was profoundly impressed by her 'wonderland of beautiful paintings' and wrote: 'Imagine being surrounded [by] Ben Nicholson, David Jones, Boudin, Seurat and other French impressionists. Talk about elevating one's spirits !!' Later still, he wrote how Helen 'uplifted my soul and made me think with a new sense of purity'. Eventually, Nicholson owned Kelly's *Dockray*, which may, like *The Barn at Cockley Moor,* have been painted for Miss Sutherland but was certainly a tangible sign of their shared experience of this isolated cultural paradise. Kelly was an admirer too of David Jones' calligraphy which he enjoyed at Cockley Moor and which bears similarities to his own capitalised inscriptions, such as STRANDS, the name of Joan David's house, which is illustrated here. The attractive style of Kelly's handwriting, which won him a prize at school, enhances the appeal of his letters. Nicholson's hand, in contrast, was so appallingly illegible that T.S. Eliot required him to type his verse.

In the Nicholson letters Kelly refers to the struggle of the artist. Notions of his battle against critics, philistines and the complacency of the affluent bourgoisie elicit the statement to Nicholson that 'it is great news that you carry on the good fight'. His struggle is clearly bound up with the feeling that although things may be tough at times, it is all very worthwhile and that he senses 'something very precious' in his work. Kelly seems blissfully unaware of the battle that many of these groups felt that they were having with him. Both artist and poet were, in their very different ways, prepared to persevere and to 'give it Wigan', a popular local phrase meaning try your utmost, with which Kelly signs off one of his letters and which Nicholson uses in his poem *At the Musical Festival*.

Not all their interests were shared. Through his organist stepmother, Nicholson became interested in music and wrote musically inspired verse such as *For the Grieg Centenary*. The artist did not show an equivalent interest in music, predictably disliking pop and hating folk; however, he loved the singing of Nat King Cole. Sport was much more important to Kelly who was a considerable footballer until he was forty years old, a keen member of Marron Cycling Club and a successful cricketer. He and his twin brother John would often open the batting for the Post Office team. Nicholson, having had TB, was less physically robust but took a great interest in cricket and describes the sport in detail in *Provincial Pleasures*.

Financially, Nicholson was in a stronger position than Kelly for the duration of their relationship as he had inherited his parents' house, had an income from his publications and readings and his wife Yvonne worked as a teacher. Kelly, once he had left the Post Office in 1958 led a more precarious existence, though supported in part by his two wives in turn. Still, after the 1950s he always managed to run a car which is perhaps an indication that his circumstances were not quite as poverty-stricken as he sometimes made out. Another major difference between them was that Nicholson was 'as confined as a limpet' in Millom, while Kelly was unsettled and lived in a variety of places in Cumberland, Pembrokeshire and Norfolk. In Wales and East Anglia, he expressed a strong sense of nostalgia, pined for the 'sharply etched' fells and called himself 'an alien in a foreign land'. Consequently, Kelly re-cycled his memories in his letters, not only for posterity but also as a palliative. In contrast, Nicholson benefited from his continual and reassuring proximity to the Millom community which he held in great affection. The artist's psychological complexities led to a divorce from both his wives, Audrey James and Christine Griffiths, whereas the poet married late and lived happily with his wife Yvonne Gardner for the duration of her life.

We know what they both looked like but not from portrait paintings. Nicholson has been honoured with busts by Josefina de Vasconcellos and Joan Palmer while in his portrait photographs by Cressida Pemberton-Pigott and Christopher Barker, with his superb whiskers, he looks genial and relaxed. There are also several fine mature photographs of Kelly, working with assurance on his etching press and others by Clive Cooke. Workington has not yet celebrated Kelly's achievement with a memorial but his ashes were scattered on the shore below Lanthwaite Green, near his beloved Loweswater. Nicholson has a fine window by Christine Boyce in St. George's church, Millom, where he lies in its adjacent churchyard.

Kelly's paintings and letters, with Nicholson's verse and prose, are the vectors which enabled their individual reputations to survive into the present century. In 2007, Nicholson is a better known figure throughout Cumbria and in the national cultural community via the Faber edition of *Collected Poems* (1994) and his recent entry by Anthony Thwaite in the Oxford Dictionary of Biography, but he still awaits a full-scale biographer. The recent founding of the Norman Nicholson Society has provided a forum for both scholars and enthusiasts who are determined to consolidate his position. Kelly has, since his death, been the focus of three illustrated publications and of several commercial exhibitions at Castlegate Gallery, Cockermouth. The volumes have accumulated valuable biographical material and critical observations but it would now be worthwhile to locate the paintings sold in his lifetime and to assimilate the scattered texts of his vast correspondence. Devotees of the cultural geography of Cumbria await such developments in both Nicholson and Kelly studies.

David A. Cross   Carlisle, August 2007

Peartree Cottage Letterhead

Road to St. David's from Fishguard

Letters From Levens

Harbour, Workington

Levens Park Cottage,
Sedgwick,
KENDAL,
Westld.

Sunday [   ] May 1971

Dear Norman and Yvonne,

Christine and I spent a wonderful and exciting day today wandering along the byways in and around Dentdale. We enjoyed our visit to Millom and thank you for such kind hospitality. Looking forward to your visit here.

Kindest regards,
Percy and Christine

In this transcript, cuts have been made which eliminate details considered superfluous by the present author who would be glad to hear from readers with further letters from Kelly to Nicholson. Square brackets indicate additions made to improve the clarity, while round brackets are Kelly's own. As Kelly's illustrations do not always relate to the text of the letters that follow them, some of the present images have been taken from other sources.

Greysouthern

Levens Park Cottage,   Tuesday morning [1971]

Dear Norman,

        Thank you for your letter which arrived this a.m. Couldn't resist penning the
above. I began sorting out the mess of work in the barn on Sunday and discovered a batch of 30"
x 22" drawings, my first on leaving the Postal Service in '58. Hadn't seen them for at least ten
years, so on looking thro' I was almost moved to tears. The feeling of loneliness in some of the
subject matter is almost frightening & I was amazed at the quality of drawing. They were too
much for Chris, who appropriately enough was the first person to see them.

In retrospect, it was a great mistake to go to Art College in '61 but I was pushed into getting a
teaching degree to earn a living. Chris and I met far too late in life. [However,] I have no regrets
because life has to unfold in its own mysterious way. At least I have always tried to be myself and
have avoided trying to popularise any imagery. Chris is the first person to understand and to
believe this to be right !! But I am going on and I must stop. Friday would be perfect, so we hope
you can both come. We pray that Yvonne is well again.

                        Kindest thoughts and wishes from us both,
                                            Percy

---

*Kelly's dark charcoal drawings and sombre paintings are indeed somewhat harrowing and are partly a reflection of his troubled psychology. In
PK/NN 15th December 1973 he says 'I love the dark landscape' and notes that 'people have been fascinated by my black and white work but
found it too strong to live with'. The powerful dark drawings gave another correspondent, Jimmy Cartmel, 'a sense of forboding' (letter to Joan
David 16.11.89). Chris Wadsworth suggests that they were the result of his traumatic 're-birth' on leaving the postal service (2004 p.82).*

Docks, Barrow-in-Furness

Levens Park Cottage,   Friday 14 May 1971

Dear Norman,

       Whilst busying with breakfast things this morning Chris remarked 'I hope the postman brings something interesting'. She had just finished speaking when 'clank' went the letter box and hey presto, I held up your card triumphantly - much more valued than a monetary prize !

We travelled to Dent via Kirkby Lonsdale (the ice cream and hot dog vendors were busy ensconced by the delectable bridge) and thence to Barbon. Weekenders [were] everywhere so we turned left along the B6255 and left again at Hawes, stopping here and there to pencil notes. From Garsdale Head we went over a gorgeous and spectacular moor road back again to Dent. Picnickers had vacated the bridge, so I did some drawing [but] the breeze was chilling. My eyes are not what they were, so I have to use a mechanical aid, a camera. Chris, bless her, bludgeoned me into buying a moderately priced single [lens] reflex effort about twelve months ago and now we have an interesting collection of slides.

I hope you will permit me to send more decorated notes from time to time as we wander around. Chris was very touched by your kind remark. She is a very kind and wonderful person. The gift of bread & jam was typical of her. We hope your Newcastle reading goes well.

Regards,
Percy

As a hypochondriac, Kelly often complained about his eyes and often wore tri-focals (letter to Joan David 28.3.84); He used a camera for recording buildings about to be destroyed by development; Nicholson gave many readings in public. (See PK/NN Saturday 30th [December] 1978 and note).

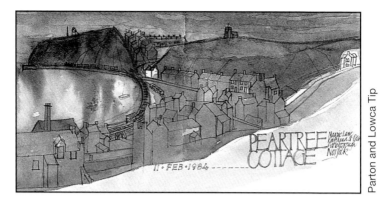

Parton and Lowca Tip

Levens Park Cottage,   June 1971

Dear Norman and Yvonne,

              Chris and I travelled to West Cumberland yesterday to pick up some things left behind. Amongst a pile of books Chris was delighted to find our copy of *Rock Face*. I say 'our' because it is a book shared and loved especially on winter evenings. The incident reminded me to write to you.

We were all set to go out into the country on Saturday. The mini was packed with paints and paper, when suddenly, the telephone bell jangled. Chris dashed into the cottage to answer the dastardly thing, then out she came [to announce that a friend was to visit]. My heart sank, for I was so excited at the thought of going out into the landscape. It was a heavenly day - dark and light, the greens vibrant, the sky with clouds grey- mauve, the sun at times appearing with a soft radiant light. I thought of the wild mustard and the fields of buttercups and the hills and the farms and cottages. [Our friend] eventually arrived but all the while he was with us my heart kept longing for the landscape. He left around five thirty and half an hour later Chris and I were on top of Farleton Fell. I did some interesting drawing and although it was cold, I persevered until dusk. It is lovely country hereabouts but my heart is in Cumberland.

On our visit yesterday my heart kept missing a beat now and again. There is a kind of magic and strength even in a bit of scraggy country... perhaps one feels a sympathy and kinship for the good solid people who eke out a living. One is [often] aware of the persistent wind. The waste tip at Lowca is now an ugly shape, pate smooth, the unreal green grass crew cut. Towards the end of our lease at Distington, we looked over a farmhouse and barn which was up for sale. Unfortunately, we had no money, which was a pity. Parton beach fascinates us both. Here we collected tons of sea coal and made friends with some of the old characters, ex miners, who frequent the beach. Tears were shed when we went down one day to bid [them] goodbye. I have enormous respect for miners, steelworkers & dalesmen.

My main reason for writing is to tell you how much we are both looking forward to your visit to the cottage. Do please come soon and in spite of what I scribbled on pages 1 & 2 [above] I would not mind when you called !!

                            Kindest regards,
                            Percy and Chris

Nicholson's Rock Face *(1948) is 'a less celebrated work' (Philip Gardner,* Norman Nicholson, *Twayne English Authors, 1973 p.62-3);*
Farleton Fell lies between Levens and Kirkby Lonsdale; Lowca tip appears in the distance in From Parton to Lowca with Moresby Church
(illustrated Burkett and Rickerby p.92, also see opposite); This composition was repeated several times and one version is in the Government
National Collection (Wadsworth 2007 unpaginated: about p.86); Like Whitehaven from above St James's Church *(Abbot Hall Art*
Gallery), an example of his love of looking down from a high vantage point to buildings by the coast. In PK/NN 30.12.78 he regrets that
the view of St David's from the high ground is spoiled by bungalows; Before Levens, PK lived at Distington; Exposed strata of coal under the
sea gradually erode and deposit pieces of coal on the beach. Nicholson refers to collecting coal in Cleator Moor.

Engine, Hodbarrow

Levens Park Cottage,   Thursday 11 a.m.
                                                                      [probably later in June 1971]

Dear Norman and Yvonne,

        A note in haste. We are taking the children to see the steam engine
collection at Carnforth. Your letter just received. We will be delighted to see you both [and]
understand you wanting to get back in the daylight. We [also] dislike driving in the dark. It is
arduous and worse, one cannot see the landscape !! You are welcome to come anytime. What about
lunch ? The park is lovely just now. Looking forward to your company.

        Percy and Chris and the children

Whitehaven from above St. James' Church

Levens Park Cottage,   Tuesday 22 June 1971

Dear Norman,

On returning from Milnthorpe via a back road I did the above sketch. These bridges are lovely creations. Two miles from the cottage we discovered a scrap dump and in it we found a huge clump of red poppies, the domesticated variety, white foxgloves of lovely proportions, columbine (mauve) and honeysuckle. Needless to say we collected a large bouquet!! and stuffed an old oak chair on the roof rack and some wire grid, to make into a seive for ashes. What a pair we are.

Now to your letter, which needless to say gave us enormous pleasure. Your visit was a joy and I am glad you were able to find a whiff of West Cumberland in the cottage. It was kind of you to send the poem - it means a great deal to us both. Chris remarked since meeting you, your poems mean so much more and she hangs onto every line. I intend doing a study from a Hodbarrow sketch, pen the words and frame it. We shall bring it along on our next visit to Millom.

I spent a wonderful day, five winters ago, painting near Bowland Bridge. A friend of mine, born in Windermere (his father was a boat builder and his mother a friend of Beatrix Potter) & now exiled in Cornwall where he runs a painting school, accompanied me. I remember it was a quiet, sad day, [with] no cars. I remarked to Charles, 'We are fortunate mortals. Here we are amongst nature, in perfect accord, over there is a jungle called civilisation with all its stress, jealousies and too much hate'. Later we picked snowdrops. I still have the two paintings but I am very jealous about my work & sadly I put them away out of sight of Charles. Sounds bad after the foregoing, but I have experienced too much copying in the past !

There is an antique shop [in Dent] so we had a ten minute browse. The antique man turned out to be a collector of railway bric-a-brac and during conversation came back with a fabulous old engineering book [with] super old drawings of cranes, engines, bridges. I wanted to ask him if I could borrow the book but he wasn't the sort of person who could be so generous. Some day we must organise a show of colour slides. I have 30 taken in and around Millom and perhaps 300 depicting Whitehaven, Maryport, fell country farms and bridges. Let the slides do the talking. Some are very beautiful. A friend, who is a professional photographer, said some complimentary things about them.

[Others say] 'Your life must be one long holiday'. Little do folk realise the hazards one has to face. Only on rare days am I perfectly well. According to Dame Laura Knight this is the fate of the artist.

Bless you both and thank you for accepting our meagre table. Thank you too for the information regarding Cumberland ore.

Percy

Charles Breaker (1906-1985) ran the Newlyn Holiday Sketching Group from 1949-65, where PK taught in the 1950s; He is conscious of his own hypocrisy here. It was Breaker who encouraged Kelly to move south and as Cornwall was too expensive, he settled on Wales. Breaker, who introduced Mary Burkett to PK (letter to Joan David 27.7.83), liked PK's marmalade enhanced with extra lemon juice and demerara sugar (letter to Joan David 16.6.1983); In the diary of 1978 Kelly illustrated snowdrops (Wadsworth 2004 p.44); Hodbarrow, the source of much of Millom's iron ore, is referred to in Nicholson's Wednesday Early Closing *(pp.134-6) and is called Odborough in his* Provincial Pleasures; *The Hodbarrow poem referred to here may have been* Bee Orchid at Hodbarrow *(Curry p.276); The photographer here is probably Clive Coote. (See PK/NN late summer 1971); Dame Laura Knight (1877-1970) the English painter.*

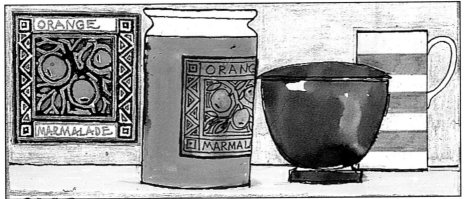

Marmalade Jar

Blast Furnace, Millom (a sad epitaph)

Levens Park Cottage,

Dear Norman,

It was so kind of you to send the plant identification. What a super name. The time is now six and the sun has been shining for almost two hours. My father aged 87, my two elder sisters and brother-in-law travelled over to see us yesterday and we all had such an enjoyable time. They brought lots of food. Muriel, the youngest (58) is a superlative cook and has a terrific sense of fun. She is in charge of the Lillyhall School canteen, her husband is the caretaker, and she had us in tears recounting amusing incidents. My father, bless him, is so boyish in spite of his years. Before setting out on a walk he called me out and gave me an old envelope whispering 'Put it away and don't let the others know !'

After they had departed, we discovered the envelope contained ten pound notes. We do appreciate his help because being a joiner all his working life, (he retired on his eightieth birthday), he never earned a great deal of money. I find his conversation fascinating because he recalls so vividly the period before and during the two World Wars. I asked him specifically about the Lowca Engine Works because there is a section [about it] in the book *The Lake District at Work*. He remembered it well. Father has always been a Methodist but I was brought up a [member of the] Plymouth Brethren, of the strictest kind. My grandparents both belonged to this sect. Before the engine works closed down they built flat-bottomed boats in steel, which were exported to Africa. My brother-in-law remarked that during a journey from Maryport to Distington he counted 116 chimneys. The world certainly has changed. Remember all the exciting smells of those yesterdays or yesteryears !!

The children send their thanks for the nuts which I forgot to mention in my last note.

Kindest thoughts from us both,
Percy

PK's sisters were Sally and Muriel. Sally, who looked after their father Oscar Kelly at this date, had previously machined and hand embroidered children's clothes. Muriel was married to Henry Brennan; J.D.Marshall and M. Davies-Shiel, The Lake District at Work: Past and Present, *David and Charles, Newton Abbot, 1976 pp.88-89. Kelly borrowed the composition of his illustrations* Blast Furnace, Millom *and* Annie Pit *(both reproduced here) from* The Lake District at Work, *the latter being labelled* Jane Pit.

Barge by the Thames near Battersea

Levens Park Cottage,

[later summer 1971]

Dear Norman & Yvonne,

It was so kind of you both to remember Chris and I whilst you journeyed across the water ! We were so touched and oft times tried to visualise the Errigal mountain, for you sounded so excited about its visual impact. Since we last met, we have travelled to Cornwall and London. It was really a business trip because I was asked by some people who live in Wimbledon to paint a picture and to see where it would hang. So kindly, they asked us to stay for a week. We decided to return after four days because the inactivity was unbearable for us both. London is no place to be, although I must say we dug out some exciting places on our wandering.

Now this place we loved. To the left of the barge is situated a small church [which] was very interesting but it was impossible to 'see' it [as] buildings and the river blocked the way and the door was locked in an unfriendly fashion. William Blake was buried in the churchyard. [I made a drawing but when] I had finished, it lacked body, so I grabbed the ketchup bottle (we were in a very sleazy cafe drinking tea) and sprinkled it over the paper. Dipping my fingers in the left-over tea, I created a wash drawing. Apparently some of the clientele saw my antics and were fascinated. Do you know, the sauce produced a lovely colour, albeit somewhat aromatic !!

We called on the young photographer Clive Coote, who [had] stayed with us over Easter and spent two super evenings talking and looking at slides, including a great many studies of me not posed. I thought I would be embarassed to see them but, on the contrary, I found them fascinating, especially those which showed me working. Clive has a studio in Chelsea and on the second evening, time passed so pleasantly, we left at 5.30 a.m. !! primarily because we missed the last bus and we walked to Wimbledon !! It was lovely and warm in the early dawn.

The children re-start school next week, so we shall be coming over to Millom on the first good day. It will be exciting to see Hodbarrow again and, I pray, your two good selves.

Kindest wishes from us all,
Percy and Chris

Errigal is a distinctive pointed mountain in Co. Donegal. According to David Cooper, this is the only evidence of Nicholson having travelled to Ireland; Blake was actually buried at the Dissenters' Burial Ground at Bunwell Fields, today near Old Street Station; Another version of this ketchup story appears in a letter to Joan David 25.5.1983 (illustrated Wadsworth 2004 p.87); PK sometimes used unusual pigments such as blackberry juice or food colouring (letter Joan David 16.7.1990). Once, at Parton, he forgot his water bottle and made do with salt water which 'takes longer to dry' (undated letter to Joan David in present author's collection); Clive Coote has had a long and successful career in photography both of industrial archaeology, publishing Remains of a Revolution with Anthony Burton (Deutsch, 1975), and more recently of cinema stills for Iris and Notting Hill. He corresponded with Kelly from 1970-1982, following their meeting on the bridge at Allonby when Coote was taking photographs for a piece in the Telegraph on Charles Dickens' tour of West Cumbria. Once, Kelly took Coote with him for tea with Nicholson in Millom and the photographer observed to the present author how the artist held the poet in 'reverence'. Always having been promised a painting as a gift by Kelly, Coote eventually bought one at Castlegate Gallery; Kelly kept extraordinary hours, as Joan David discovered on one of her visits to Norfolk (Wadsworth 2004 p.53).

Levens Park Cottage,   18 October 71

Dear Norman and Yvonne,

I have fussed about with this drawing for ages. The old tug is taken from an equally old photograph in *Cumberland Iron*, a fascinating book about the beginning and end of Hodbarrow Mine. It must have been a hive of activity during the late nineteenth and twentieth centuries. What a mass of steamers and sailing craft sailed to and fro from Borwick rails !! Together with our photographer friend Clive Coote, we travelled over to Hodbarrow about three weeks ago and spent a fascinating day. There was a steamer, Antwerp registered, taking on a load of scrap at the end of the pier. By chance we met a [manager] supervising the loading. He gave me permission to take any wheel patterns from the old foundry and to wander about the Steel Works [where] Clive took a series of photographs (industrial) for the Sunday Telegraph.

Tug Boat *Duddon*

One place on [his] list was Hebden Bridge and [another] Bingley, Yorkshire [then] we came home via Haworth, another unvisited place. How commercialised it was, [with] gift and antique shops everywhere. On a walk to Top Withens we discovered a lovely old table upside down in a disused quarry. With an effort, because I wasn't feeling too well at this stage, we dragged it half a mile to our faithful A35 and plonked it on the roof rack. It now resides in the kitchen !! Clive arrived at a convenient time because some friends had invited us to a private viewing at Lancaster University and we couldn't think how to get out of it. There was [also] to be a poetry reading of a dubious type, so we were spared this too. I may be wrong but I believe it takes a rare talent to produce poetry of the sort which we prefer. [This] may sound old hat but we prefer to worship beauty.

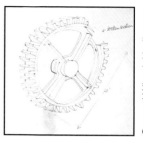

Cogged Wheel, Hodbarrow

Now to your letter. The week after our proposed visit was one of lovely sunny days. The children were all off school [and] I well remember saying to Chris: 'what a great pity we cannot go over to Millom'. We have no friends here about so it was with regret that we were unable to see the TV programme which you mentioned. It was most kind [of you] to think of purchasing one of my efforts. I shall certainly get some things together for you to see.

While Clive was here we had a particularly happy evening playing conkers [with the children]. You will be happy to know we read some of your poetry and altogether we had a wonderful weekend. I was constantly reminded of Cicero's words:

> Friendship is nothing else than an accord
> in all things, human and divine conjoined
> with mutual good will and affection.

> Kindest regards from us all,
> Percy and Chris

p.s. Had a letter published in last week's Westmorland Gazette which will make me not a little unpopular.

P.

Alan Harris, Cumberland Iron: The Story of Hodbarrow Mine 1855-1968, Barton, 1970; Though evidently not of great interest to Kelly, Top Withens was the inspiration for Emily Brontë's Wuthering Heights; PK was a keen scavenger and picked up much of his furniture in this way. Once he salvaged furniture from a Guy Fawkes bonfire (letter to Joan David 4.5.1983) and in Wales, Christine rescued a pine wash stand from a dump; One of the wheel patterns he took is illustrated here. The original is in the Abbot Hall collection (donated by Rob David); This reference to Marcus Tullius Cicero (106-43 B.C.), is from On Friendship (VI. xx) and is one of Kelly's periodic self-conscious literary references. The same words appear on a pale sheet of calligraphy (Wadsworth 2004 p.48); According to David Ralli, Kelly's last words were about friendship (Burkett and Rickerby p.88); His letter appeared in the Westmorland Gazette of 15th October 1971 in which he criticises the excessive idealism of the director of the new Kendal and District Arts and Community Centre (now The Brewery Arts Centre).

Maryport Harbour

Levens Park Cottage,   Tuesday 30 Nov 1971

Dear Norman and Yvonne,

You will be happy to know I have put a gold frame round the Maryport painting. I am sure you will enjoy it. The St Bees effort had to stay put for it was impossible to get over to W. Cumberland to make further studies. [Recently] Allen Freer called with his wife and two delightful daughters. Frankly he was flabbergasted with my work. 'Joseph Herman [and] Lowry, are knocked into a cocked hat', - flattery indeed! Apparently, he did not come to buy because he had spent all on a David Jones watercolour but asked me to put two small things away which he will collect in the spring. He also took away a folio of prints. He mentioned my work to Geoffrey Green [of] Tib Lane Gallery Manchester & he hot-footed to Levens the day after. He bought a print and asked if I could put on an exhibition this coming March. He [also] wanted to buy your painting of Maryport !! Allen has spread my name around so we are to be visited by another gallery owner, plus two collectors (wealthy ones) from Yorkshire.

I mentioned all this to Mary Burkett and she came right away. I was then introduced [by her] to Peter Scott who has gone literally overboard and has commissioned me to do a large painting of Kendal. See what you have started !! I told Allen that we wanted a lithographic press and he said he wouldn't stop [selling prints] until he had obtained enough money [for me] to buy the press. Peter Scott is going to provide accommodation in the Provincial Insurance building to house my roughs and press !!

We shall pop over with the painting soon I hope. I know we shall both enjoy the journey and meeting you both again. I have just finished an interpretation of a Persian painting, a battle scene. Molly Lefebure finds slight overtones of Uccello in my work and it is interesting to note that I carried a small reproduction of Uccello's *San Marco* with me right through the war years. I have an idea Mary Burkett might buy this Persian effort, perhaps not. The delicate washes and almost abstract shapes, shape within shape, is most satisfying to me at any rate.

We send our kindest regards,

Yours,
Percy and Chris

Allen Freer is an artist and was then an Inspector of Schools in Manchester, who invited poets to speak to teachers. He introduced Norman Nicholson to Percy Kelly; L.S.Lowry (1887-1976) visited Kelly at Glen Cottage on one of his visits to see the Cumbrian artist Sheila Fell (1931-1979) and Kelly wrote: 'he was in fact an intruder [and I] disliked the man's inflated ego'. (large undated letter to Joan David in present author's collection; also see Wadsworth 2004 p.61 and 106); Josef Herman (b.1911) was a Polish emigré artist who came to Britain c.1940; David Jones (1896-1974) was much encouraged by Helen Sutherland (1881-1965), see introduction. Allen Freer's purchase is now at the Harris Art Gallery, Preston; Geoffrey Green (d. c. 2003) ran the Tib Lane Gallery, near Deansgate in Manchester for many years and on visiting Kelly was very annoyed that he refused to agree to an exhibition; PK produced posters and invitation card designs for the first Persian exhibition for Mary Burkett, then Director of Abbot Hall Art Gallery, Kendal; He also bought an etching press from Sidney Buckley (d.1982), a Lake Artists Society exhibitor from 1948-81 (Jane Renouf, The Lake Artists Society, 2004 p.155). At Carlisle Art College he worked on lithography; Peter Scott, Chairman of the Provincial Insurance Company (1957-77) and later chairman of the Trustees of Abbot Hall was a great benefactor of, and correspondent with, Kelly; It appears that Nicholson was the catalyst of this spate of sales; Molly Lefebure, the Coleridge biographer and friend of Kelly. Uccello did not paint a work called San Marco, though he did design mosaics in St Mark's basilica. Kelly may be recalling The Rout of San Romano (National Gallery; The Louvre; Uffizi).

Parton

Levens Park Cottage,   [soon after November 30th] 1971

Dear Norman and Yvonne,

        We were overjoyed to receive your letter containing such wonderful and exciting news !!!

Our journey to Millom will depend largely on the weather, so [we hope] to be coming over on this coming Friday. I want to attempt [the] large drawing from the slagbanks. We have had to suffer some rather negative company of late, so it will be good to meet you both again.

Our kindest regards,

Yours ever,
Percy and Chris

This "exciting news" is still a puzzle, but it may be a reference to Nicholson's award of a travel bursary by the Society of Authors.

Letters from St David's

7, Gospel Lane,
ST DAVID'S,
Pembrokeshire.

15 December 73

Dear Norman and Yvonne,

       I remember reading one time that a young niece of Henry Moore asked him to do a painting. The only materials to hand were some children's watercolours and wax crayons [so] the Underground studies owed everything to this chance discovery. Owing to circumstance, I am having to use a box of Winsor and Newton "Postadiscs", a reed pen, felt tips and the cheapest typing paper. [Unlike Moore,] I have discovered little to advantage. [From here,] a few feet up a ladder, one can look westwards over the Breton type rooftops and see the tiny fields encroaching upon Carnllidi (595 ft), one of the curious, immense rock outcrops.

Steam Engine, *Charlie*

My heart beats faster at this time of the year. I love the dark landscape: a deep sided road, a twisted hawthorn, the telling exactitude of a black perpendicular telegraph pole moving t'wards the fading light … this is the whole, the universe. Physically, Pembroke and Cumberland are one; the feeling equally stimulating, but I miss the industrial pattern of Cumberland and Lorton and Crummock, Loweswater, Low Park and Buttermere & a host of other places. I have met people who have been fascinated by my black and white work but found it far too strong to live with. The Lake artist, the ordinary artist, merely skims the surface. It is my belief that the true artist whether figurative or abstract has to be part poet. To see a small part of the whole, take a part and then add a part and if this be of an indefineable quality, this is creative art in its purest form.

This leads to your interesting discourse on free verse. I agree with every word. I have heard some rotten poetry on the wireless, [with] awful grammar, no balance, crude swear words and all instant rubbish. [In contrast] I have remembered some of your verses for twenty years or more and they stay alive; [when one] sees a view, then follows the [poetic] association, especially now we are in exile.

Just below this cottage, on the Fishguard road, there is a small market garden. One day whilst Chris was purchasing vegetables, I saw the cottage with the sun above the road and it looked most poetic, 'midst lovely form. No doubt you noticed on your visit to Pembroke that the cottages have one enormous stack. The fireplaces are set in the corner of the living room which is most interesting. At the first opportunity I will make a study of one and send it to you.

Last night I was scribbling away when suddenly I glanced at the clock. 3.00 a.m. !! Our life here is quite unbalanced most [of the] time because we all have to live in one small room. I have to wait till ten p.m. before my mind can adjust to creative things in a positive way [though] the creative awareness is with me always. I remember many years ago playing soccer at Cockermouth one Saturday in December. The ground was on a piece of high ground and looking south-eastwards one could see the lovely panoramic view of the western fells. During the game, I became fascinated by the after-glow on Grasmoor's steep cliffs. For a moment I quite oblivious to the fact that I was involved in a hectic and partisan football game. My team mates thought I had gone into a trance and many a time afterwards my leg was pulled over the incident!

Strange you should refer to the T.V. in your letter because a Mr and Mrs Thomas, our local grocers, asked [us] if we would like their T.V. set, a 24 inch monster. [We] decided to say 'nay', in a gracious way, of course. 'What you don't have you don't miss.' We [do] have a battery radio, so we are not dependant upon the electric supply. How super it will be to hear your talk. We intend to make a monster memo so we can be constantly reminded of the date. I remember I was asked to get some material together with Molly Lefebure. At the time I had a tape recorder so we were able to record at great length. Molly took the tape to London and I was informed the BBC were quite impressed.

I remember a Scottish artist, Ian Fleming R.S.A., R.S.W., who had a high regard for my work in the fifties and he got a fellow academician to sponsor me for election to the R.S.W. and R.S.A. At the election I failed by a narrow margin and the late Dr Honeyman, who helped too, said: 'Your trouble is, you are a sassenach !!' That year Anne Redpath failed election too. One or two of the artists who were elected [then] have failed to stand the course, they are quite mundane and washed out. In England it doesn't seem to matter what one's nationality is.

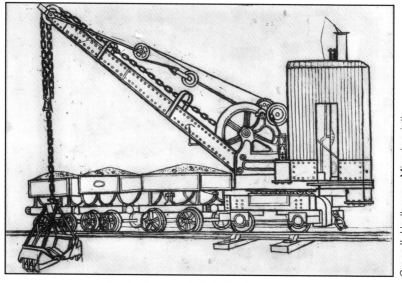

Crane II, Hodbarrow Mine (a print)

Reproduced by courtesy of Abbot Hall Art Gallery, Kendal

'Twas sad to hear about Hodbarrow, a place I have come to love over the years. It only seems yesterday when the busy little engines chuffed all over the place. I have some very early drawings, one of which I turned into an etching. [This shows] not the place but a steam crane and waggons. I remember the waggon wheels were rusted solid and they were loaded with gravel, as if they had been left in the middle of a shift and forgotten. Kathy Whitehorn has a print and I gather one hangs in the Abbot Hall Museum [of Lakeland Life] and Industry. Chris accompanied me on three drawing expeditions but, alas, each time the gentle rain from heaven began to fall, on arrival, making drawing impossible. I did try a felt pen but the fluid ran alarmingly. This is when the camera is invaluable.

How the world changes. Whitehaven and Maryport are terribly scarred. I am fortunate to have so many [of these] early drawings executed before the all-out demolition began. Workington, oddly enough, has changed very little or at least not around the dock and harbour. I wish I had worked harder and with more detail in the early days and yet, on reflection, it would have been impossible. I am sure many of the studies will have historical interest in years to come, because although I simplify a great deal, the element of truth in the buildings [makes them] more acceptable than very early paintings and prints. The drawing of the winding engine at St Helen's Colliery c.1968 ought to have been kept in the county [but] it was reproduced in the Irish Times in a rather splendid way. The original had immense feeling of simple elementary strength. The day after the pit closed, the vandals got to work [and] every bit of brass was removed, plastic sheeting and copper piping suffer[ing] the same fate.

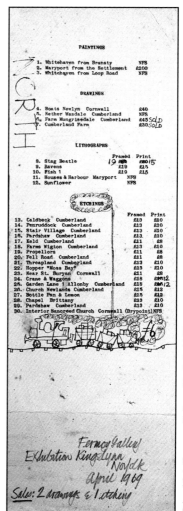

Price List, Fermoy Gallery, Norfolk 1969

I end this letter with the copy of a sketch I did in early March, a lovely area two miles from St David's. Masses of exuberant golden yellow gorse, new grasses and new flowers. The paper restricts me but I pray that it gives you pleasure along with the other decoration. I feel flattered that you thought fit to frame my previous letter. We loved yours and I hope again this effort in the form of a monster Christmas greeting will bring to you a feeling of good fellowship.

Love and blessings to you from us all,
Percy, Chris, Andy and Nicky

Henry Moore (1898-1986) the British sculptor, as an official war artist (1940-42), produced drawings of figures sleeping on the London Underground; Kelly would add telegraph poles to 'add strength' to his compositions (letter to Joan David 5.5.83) while Nicholson also includes the motif in Wales; Grasmoor is a fell 2791 feet high, above Crummock Water; Having rejected T.V. in Wales, once alone in Norfolk, Kelly became a keen (and critical) watcher of T.V. while Nicholson, in his later years, would lie in bed watching the cricket; Molly Lefebure reports that she still has this tape but that it was never intended for the BBC; The artists Ian Fleming (1906-1990) and William Burns (1921-1972) put him up for this election; Dr Tom Honeyman (1894-1971), the dynamic director of Kelvin Grove Gallery, Glasgow (see letter to Joan David 13.8.1984); Anne Redpath, the artist (1895-1965); Katharine Whitehorn, the popular journalist, then with The Observer and now with Saga magazine has a print of a steam train (illustrated here, page 33); 'the gentle rain from heaven' is from Shakespeare's The Merchant of Venice *Act IV scene i; Kelly described how vandalism and arson destroyed the unusual Back Brow Methodist church in Maryport which had a squat hexagonal tower (illustrated here p.12); The St Helen's Colliery was between Siddick and Flimby; John Fitzmaurice Mills wrote in the Irish Times in September 1968 how when etching Kelly 'draws out of the plate a coarse strength that hitches itself to the nature of its subject' (cited Burkett and Rickerby); Andy and Nicky are Christine Griffiths' younger children by her first husband.*

Pica, near Distington

7, Gospel Lane,   6 September 1975

Dear Norman and Yvonne,

        About a fortnight ago we had a surprise visit from Allen Freer. During the conversation he mentioned that you were awaiting a reply to a letter written ages ago. This put me in a quandary because before Christmas I despatched to you a sumptuously decorated envelope in a long and equally decorated letter. Consequently, I too waited patiently. I do know at least two decorated envelopes to other people were never received and I wonder if the one sent to you suffered a similar fate?

[By July] we had to get our gallery going in order to make some money. I managed to get some energy from somewhere and worked jolly hard until last weekend when we finally opened [it as] the Gospel Lane Gallery. Because of the late opening we have missed the holiday season and only a handful of people have called to look around. A pity because we have created a most beautiful room [though much] of the paint and materials came from the dump, discarded by RAF Brandy. One day Mr Auld, Keeper of the Glasgow Galleries knocked at the door to compliment us on our handiwork. We have had a score of such compliments and in a lecture about the preservation of old buildings in Wales, Elizabeth Beasley kindly referred to our efforts. Also a vicar (retired) knocked to enquire the address of the builder who had done the work. They were really shattered when Chris said: 'You are looking at him !'

The Kendal exhibition is fixed to open next July [so] it will be a rush. Happily, I have some etchings framed and five quite large and beautiful watercolours. Two of the paintings (30 x 22 inches) are studies of the Pembroke landscape and were painted very recently. When seen together they will be very interesting. Although they have extended my palette [they] seem to possess the mystery of our Cumberland light and yet are essentially Wales. Last weekend, in spite of a mass of holiday folk, [I] managed a large painting of a beach near St David's. I had only two inks, blue-black and brown but the effect was stimulating. At the same beach I did some drawing of the cliffs. The cliff scenery hereabouts is splendid but rarely interests me because the geometry is wrong. The sun shone warm [and it was] quite unreal, after spending two years or more building, to be able to go out and let one's mind wander. There is not one village paintable [here, however] and the landscape is ever the resentful lover, ever sad.

I framed eight watercolours which would show in any company and then printed and framed about twenty prints [which] depicted the lighter side of my character: eleven plant forms, engines and one interesting plate showing a road and a Pembrokeshire dwelling. Looking back it is amazing what I have achieved. I even scraped and repainted the old etching press and how splendid it looks in the workshop. Visitors to the gallery from England were infatuated by the strong northern scene. It makes it all worthwhile when a person shows some measure of appreciation. I spoke of Hodbarrow today to one visitor [and] your name cropped up and my heart warmed when she remarked: 'How exciting. I know his work so well.'

A few nights ago, when doing studies of the cathedral, I had to speak to some boys who were throwing sods at each other, shrieking like wild things. I tried to put it across that this was sacred ground and that one ought to show respect. I am supposed to have a permit issued by the Dean to work in the precincts of the cathedral [as was required] in Great Broughton where I was hauled over the coals for not seeking permission. [Later, when] I produced post cards, the church council demanded a royalty of one penny per card.

I must tell you [that] Claude and Audrey Harrison called on us in August quite out of the blue. It appears they have recently bought some property near Haverfordwest. [This] made me quite homesick and [feel] quite old since we last met at a meeting of the Lake Artists in 1961.

We all pray that you are both well and happy and full of creative thoughts.

Love and blessings,
Percy, Chris, Andy and Nicki

———————————————

This letter is from the John Rylands Library, Manchester University ms NCNI/ 1/ 158/ 1; According to Christine Mills, the Gospel Lane Gallery was only open for three weeks, soon reverting to storage space; Alasdair Auld, Keeper from 1956-88; Claude Harrison is a prominent member of the Lake Artists Society who specialises in allegorical compositions of clowns and magicians. His wife Audrey painted meticulous flower paintings which would have appealed to both Nicholson and Kelly (Renouf cited above pp. 166-7 and 180-81).

Farm below Naddle Fell (a print)

7, Gospel Lane,   1st October 1976

My Dear Norman and Yvonne,

At last I have got round to scribbling some lines to you both. I can tell you we have both thought so much about you since our return. On the second day back, Brian, a young man from Newbury, who was staying in the next cottage, asked if he could come to talk to me one evening. He was fascinated by the process of etching. We talked about metals, glass making, industrial archaeology and surprisingly, poetry. Imagine my delight when he said that his favourite poet was no other than your good self. The reason, your use of words and integrity. In the anthology they had at his school, your poems were utilised for 'O' level English. When I told him you were a good friend of mine, he nearly fell off his chair. One day we must fuse our work for the whole world to see and read !

It was very kind of you to send the cutting from The Guardian. As far as I [had been] aware the exhibition went unnoticed and unsung. Not that this bothers me because the enthusiasm shown by you both and your [purchase] of the lovely wash drawing (you have good taste) [are] sufficient acknowledgement. Chris was very depressed about the lack of press coverage, so when your letter arrived she was over the moon. Unlike Constable, I never make studies of landscape or skies. They are purely imaginative, hinged upon a few pencil notes.

The local homespun architecture is deadly dull here, there is only one design [of cottage]. Originally there must have been literally thousands [of them] but all are almost fallen down or completely altered to be used as second homes. There is only one perfect specimen and it is to be found in the village of Nevern, near Cardigan. After [its owner's] day it will go the way of all the others.

On our way north to hang the work, [after] we reached Lancaster, the land towards Bowland looked very green. The sky was overcast black and grey, the dark trees and the base grey fell framing the green fields highlighted by white farmsteads took my breath away. Home. The first time I had really been moved by landscape for many a long day. What then is the mystery ? I believe that it is the linear [structure], almost wholly created by man, that gives pleasure to the mind and eye. A wall going up and up almost to touch the sky then across a satisfying slope, [then] a dramatic plunge into a ghyll to trail down again with the sureness of a controlled pencil line. The event takes place in seemingly unlimited space and the placing of a simple barn is part of the whole, the interest to spark off one's emotional sensibilities.

You may remember that during the London private view, people made their farewells and I was left alone on the pavement to find my way back to Surbiton by Tube. Not so at the Fermoy Gallery in 1969 at Kings Lynn. The gallery director organised a small group and we had dinner together. It was a very happy event.

Since we arrived back here with the pictures, it has rained almost continually and for a period it was quite torrential. The same weather that flooded Polperro. Pembrokeshire experiences more bad weather than anywhere in Britain except perhaps Cape Wrath. This summer the fog horns never stopped blowing and the signal to call out the lifeboat crew went off practically every other day. They collect in St David's and are then transported in a van to the lifeboat station, rather like the Keystone Cops.

Thank you for your kind invitation to stay.

Love from us all,
Percy, Chris, Andy and Nicki

This letter is at The John Rylands Library, Manchester University ms NCNI/1/158/2; Review by Merete Bates of the Abbot Hall exhibition, The Guardian 18th August 1976; John Constable (1776-1837) the important English landscape painter; Kelly sold two drawings and one etching at the Fermoy Gallery exhibition; Polperro in Cornwall was flooded earlier in 1976; The Keystone Cops were comic characters from the Silent Movies of Mack Sennett from 1912-17, familiar from their manic dashing about to crime scenes; Kelly did not take up Nicholson's offer to stay.

7, Gospel Lane,   Saturday 30th [December] 1978

My Dear Norman and Yvonne,

        I am so sorry that I was unable to enclose a note with the greeting card. Regarding our move to Norfolk, the cottage will be advertised in the spring and glad we will be to be rid of this place. Do you know, we will have been here six years, come March.

We have some good friends in Leicester who have commissioned me to do a large Whitehaven painting. Tony Maufe, with whom we stayed [in Norfolk], has ordered two paintings to be taken from sketches which he liked and, of course, David Eccles reassures me constantly he will send his friends along. We have a dream that we will manage a place in Norfolk and a less salubrious place in West Cumberland [perhaps the] Cleator Moor and Frizington area. The problem is getting a suitable place in Norfolk because we do not intend to do any more building work, no sir, time is too short!! It will be interesting to see how the Norfolk landscape affects me.

Thank you so much for *The Shadow of Black Combe*. It will be enjoyed time and time again and treasured. We specially enjoyed *Weeds*. In late March we passed through Cley towards Cromer and came across a village with the church set on high ground above the cottages. We looked at the scene from afar. I was deeply moved [and] felt as if I was back on the Solway. [A passing motorist said that] many artists had painted the scene but one in particular was so obsessed with it that he painted it hundreds of times. I was not surprised to hear this because I shall create a masterpiece. On our travels, time and time again I would get involved in conversation with complete strangers - all very charming and civilised because the talk was of antiquity and beauty. I felt for the first time in years that I had a trade mark and was recognised. [On another occasion one said to Chris] 'your husband has to be an artist with that face and wearing such gay colours'.

It is great news that you carry on the good fight, for you are constantly in our thoughts of tender affection and respect. You and I Norman are two fortunate people [as] we each have good companions and our work. Now and again I come across men who despair in that they will leave behind nothing at the end of the day. I do not go along with this [notion] because if a man is good and kind, he does affect some mortal soul who takes from him and carries [the virtue] on to the next generation. Sadly, that is not a tangible thing, like our poetry and painting. I sense something very precious, especially at this stage of my life.

[same letter]   New Year's Day [1979]

Chris and I went for a short walk after lunch hoping to enjoy a white landscape but, alas, there was no snow to be seen. Parts of St David's can look attractive viewed from the high ground but there are too many new bungalows which intrude and spoil the scene.

This time last year I began a diary, an illustrated one, and worked diligently each day for 179 days. Pictorially, many of the pages were really beautiful, being adorned with good calligraphy, but alas, it all came to a sad end. So much has to be left unsaid but I hope we can meet and talk during '79 and make up for lost time. We shall not forget your reading in Cley. I am glad you are both well and hope the arthritis will [clear] up for Yvonne.

A Happy and Prosperous New Year to you both.

With all our love,
Percy, Chris, Andy and Nicky

Kelly's choice of Norfolk was perhaps in part the result of his time spent in the county both during the war and during the Fermoy Gallery exhibition in 1969; The Leicester friends were Herald Goddard and his wife; Tony Maufe, a Norfolk architect, helped Kelly with architectural problems. He met the artist at the King's Lynn exhibition and in the 1970s worked for Johnson and Wright in Carlisle; There is some evidence that Kelly traced copies of his favourite paintings such as Whitehaven by working on a large board laid on the bath (letter to Joan David 26.9.83); David McAdam Eccles, Viscount Eccles (1904-1999) chairman of West Cumberland Silk Mills, Minister of Education, a correspondent (c.1976-82), supporter and collector of PK's work; Kelly spent huge amounts of time restoring his cottages in Wales and Norfolk, often with 'found' materials and to the detriment of his creative work; "The Shadow of Black Combe" and "Weeds" are titles of verses by Nicholson; PK here echoes the hymn 'Fight the Good Fight'; Chris Wadsworth observes that 179 days is a great axxageration. Several pages of this diary are illustrated in Wadsworth 2004 p. 42 ff.; According to letters written to his cousin Doreen Cornthwaite, in 1978 Nicholson gave readings in Oxford, Birmingham, Kendal, Preston and Lancaster and probably two in Norfolk.

7, Gospel Lane,   3rd September 1980

My Dear Norman and Yvonne,

Foxglove

After a three year search we have finally found a new home in East Anglia and hopefully on the 12th we will pack our bags and depart. We wanted to be near the coast but had to settle for a less fashionable area. This beautiful remote cottage's construction is oak-framed with clay lump, circa 17th century. The thatched roof has been replaced by pantiles and fairly recently a course of lovely brown-red brick, hard baked, was laid around the outside walls. Not one insect is to be seen [and] I still cannot believe the feeling of dryness [after the damp of Wales]. It is more suited to a poet than an artist. In the delightful garden is a large apple tree, a pear tree and the hedge sports two holly bushes, privet and lilac trees. The great architect really smiled on us.

I much prefer the Norfolk landscape which can be so much like Normandy. Then there are the mass of flint churches, never two alike. Part of the coast could be Allonby. Mind you, I do not relish the cold winters. However, a recent survey found that Norfolk is way ahead on the list of life expectancy. It is very odd that after seven years of being completely ignored here in Wales, people have wakened up to the fact that I exist. So many want paintings ! It appears that I am the only real artist in the Principality and there will be a never-to-be-filled gap when I leave ! All this via the grapevine. Of course, Chris will be missed [too] because she has made many friends through her immense gifts. She has created lots of beautiful knitwear and painted delightful flower studies.

I shall miss the local ash tip because I have found so many useful items. The gates are never locked so it is a free for all and for seven years our Norwegian wood-burning stove never went out and the fuel never cost one penny ! We expect to buy wood in Norfolk but this could be offset by cheaper food. I shall also miss the flowers because there is no doubt there is no place in Britain where flowers grow so profusely. The farmers never use insecticide, which is a real blessing. [However,] I certainly shall relish the absence of the Welsh language on television.

We think of you both often and do pray that your health is good.

Love from us both,
Percy and Chris

This letter is in The John Rylands Library, Manchester University ms NCNI/1/158/3; Kelly's boast of being 'the only real artist' in the Principality would doubtless have been challenged by artists such as his exact contemporary Sir Kyffin Williams (1918 - 2006).

Letters from Rockland

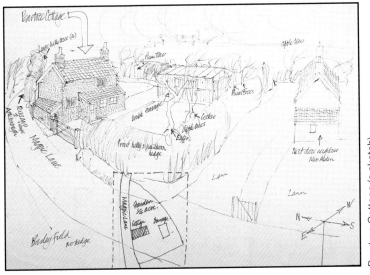

Peartree Cottage (a sketch)

Peartree Cottage,
Magpie Lane,
ROCKLAND ST PETER,
Attleborough,
Norfolk.

Saturday 11th Oct. 1980

My Dear Norman and Yvonne,

        [Above] is a very elementary sketch showing the situation of our home. Magpie Lane is a slip road leading right to the village [of Rockland St Peter] and Watton is 5 miles [away]. So we are quite remote, a stark contrast to Gospel Lane, St David's. Already we have made friends who have brought us cucumbers, tomatoes, carrots, beetroot and potatoes. [Our neighbour] Miss Alden is a lovely old soul. She is 81 years old and was born in Pear Tree [and] all her family are buried in St Peter's churchyard. You would love these people, Norman, because so many still retain old-fashioned virtues. Miss Alden's sister is the Sub-Postmistress & greengrocer. We are off to a sale of cycles tomorrow. Cycles are invaluable here because the roads are so perfect. Everyone hereabouts has a bike. Even Miss Alden pedals off every day to the church and to cook for her nephew on the Watton road.

I was delighted to read about the demand for your poetry, plus the distinction of [your] being made a Doctor of Letters by Liverpool University. Whilst I am not an egotist and never affected by publicity, I do feel [that] sincere and really talented creative souls rarely get the respect they deserve. People have come into our home and the mass of drawings and paintings strung around go unnoticed. A talented tradesman, joiner or plumber gets more [attention]. Never mind, it matters little in the end because

43

there are the few [people] that make it worthwhile. I remember when I was filmed for the BBC TV, the programme was put back for a dog show !! With regard to the Civil List [Pension], Lord Eccles [said] 'I'll put in a word at the palace'. [It] all happened because of a visit by the Director of the Arts Council. He told a friend that he had never seen such fine prints and felt that I ought to be able to work without any commercial pressures. A Civil List Pension would be a great help, as before leaving Wales I had to sell two much loved paintings. It was kind of you Norman to offer your help.

There are so many negative artists today putting on exhibitions of work [in which the] elusive indefineable quality [of the true artist] never shows. True art only bears fruit after a long objective courtship. There must be love, affection, integrity and humility. For this reason your poetry stands out. We are a dying breed and there will be none to follow. It is interesting to note that three friends who once objected to and criticised Wordsworth are now admirers of the great bard. One can denounce beauty and truth but not for long.

I was sorry, Yvonne, to be told of your indifferent health. I do pray the problem will right itself. Like Rousseau, who only felt spring in prison, it is only when one has experienced a long spell of poor health that good health is really appreciated. We hope to visit Cumberland more often because our beloved county is now much more accessible. We think of you both constantly and with the greatest affection. At least you know that you have no greater fans, Norman. The fact the Dockray picture continues to give pleasure gave me a warm glow.

Excuse the scrawl and any mistakes.

Love from us both,
Percy

[p.s.] Norfolk cottages are very pleasant indeed but if smartened up by 'settlers' they can look awfully twee. Actually, like John Betjeman, I prefer a degree of untidiness and the bits of litter. This obsession [today] with tidiness in the countryside makes it all far too sterile. I enclose this drawing, Norman, to show a comparison with the strong and simple basic structure of the Cumberland farm.

Miss Evelyn Alden (1899-1990), who had worked for Dr Barnardo's Homes, was a fine needlewoman and lived next door to Peartree Cottage. She is buried in the churchyard; Though PK claims not to be an egotist, his behaviour and statements are not infrequently egotistical; Kelly was filmed for programmes broadcast by both Border TV and Anglia; PK's aspiration for a Civil List Pension, first mooted by Aneurin Thomas, Director of the Welsh Arts Council, was not fulfilled (letter to Joan David 14, 4. 83). Nicholson refers to Wordsworth's Civil List Pension in The Five Rivers; PK's reference to Rousseau, like the Cicero quotation in PK/NN 18.10.71., is another example of his somewhat self-conscious literary references; Helen Sutherland lived at Dockray, which is mentioned in PK's letter to Rosemary Joyce after Nicholson's death (the final letter in this volume: see end note); Sir John Betjeman (1906-1984) Poet Laureate (from 1972) and architectural lobbyist whose laudatory review of one of Clive Coote's books Kelly quotes in hyperbolic detail (letter to Joan David July [C] 1983). PK sent Betjeman a drawing of Old Buckenham Church (letter to Joan David 5.6.1983). The Laureate also praised Nicholson as a 'real poet' (Daily Herald July 6th 1944 cited Gardner p.60) and accompanied him to Buckingham Palace when he collected his Queen's Medal for Poetry.

Caston Church, Norfolk

Peartree Cottage,   26th October 1982

My Dear Norman,

        I have been in a dark mood since your sad, sad letter arrived on Friday. Yvonne will always be remembered with love and affection. I wanted to grace these few words with some beautiful image as a token of my feelings. Instead, [I offer] a brief sketch of a scene I love, part of a world that has passed us by. [Nonetheless], the villagers are good folk and the church flourishes and is cared for. A gentle reminder of their fine Christian faith. I wish we lived nearer [to you] so we might help.

We both send our love and blessings,
Percy and Chris

Yvonne Nicholson (née Gardner) died on 31st August 1982;
PK's first reference to her being unwell is in the letter Tuesday morning [1971].

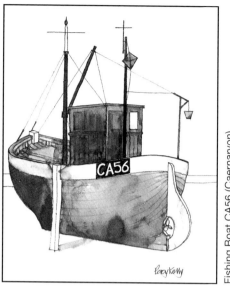

Fishing Boat CA56 (Caernarvon)

Peartree Cottage,   Monday 5th Nov. 1984

My Dear Norman,

        I cannot afford a daily newspaper or the Radio or TV Times. However, I was informed that your South Bank programme was to be screened on Sunday the fourth. I was therefore able to watch and enjoy it even in black and white. I bet it would be super in colour. I was very impressed by the photography in your programme and the direction too. [It] really did you justice, for you deserve the best. I have a tape recorder, only a cheap one. However, I was able to make a passable recording.

As you may know, Abbot Hall Gallery have a painting of mine showing Millom Steelworks. I used a lot of Red !! Before the works were demolished, I spent several days drawing and taking masses of photographs which were turned into slides.

Keep giving it 'Wigan.'

Affectionately, brother Cumbrian,
Percy

In 1973, Kelly rejected T.V. but now he has one; Melvyn Bragg's South Bank Show *on the 4th November 1984 was devoted to Nicholson. Kelly appeared on arts programme on both Border and Anglia T.V.; PK's Millom, Cumberland is still at Abbot Hall and celebrates haematite red, a colour much in evidence in West Cumbria and Furness (see* Provincial Pleasures *p.109); Florence Mine at Egremont, another source of haematite, may still be visited; The expression 'Give it Wigan', meaning 'try your utmost', was popularised by Nicholson; The words 'brother Cumbrian' are the source of the title of this present work.*

*After Norman
Nicholson died, Percy
wrote to Rosemary
Joyce, Norman's sister-
in-law.*

Peartree Cottage,   [undated 1987]

Dear Rosemary Joyce,

Thank you very much
for your letter. I am especially grateful to have
the news that the picture *Dockray* (1973) will be
in your safe-keeping and valued at the same time.

I remember after Yvonne's passing, such a sad
occasion for me, I sent a small painting of a single rose,
which I know Norman appreciated. It was an inspired
essay, so I hope it is safe. I worried about Norman being
alone because he needed to be out in the landscape. I wish I
could have lived nearer to Millom to chauffeur the dear chap up
hill and down dale. Of course, I wasn't to know that I would soon
be in the same plight. At first, when one is alone, friends come in abundance but
sadly the duration is that of an April shower, for it isn't long before you are completely alone to
fend for yourself.

Thank you for your kind offer of a book. As Norman [himself] gave me one of his books, which I
cherish, I must decline. I have, of course, got all his books of poems. I think great care will have
to be taken regarding the kind of memorial. For instance, a scented garden is not fitted for the
Cumberland climate. I was, [nonetheless] pleased to learn about the plaque.

You will be most welcome to call.

My kindest regards,
P. Kelly

---

*Rosemary Joyce is Yvonne Nicholson's sister; Dockray, the village near Cockley Moor (the home of Helen Sutherland), was a place significant to them
both and the inspiration for the verse* Cockley Moor *by Nicholson and Kelly's* Barn at Cockley Moor *which is illustrated on p.15. Winifred
Nicholson's* Cockley Moor *is in Sheffield City Art Gallery. See Val Corbett, "A Rhythm, A Rite and A Ceremony", exhibition catalogue,
Penrith Museum, 1996; Kelly also sent a drawing of a rose to David Eccles when his wife Sybil died. In* The Burning Rose, *the poet describes
a rose rather like one of Kelly's rosebuds; When Yvonne died, Nicholson lost both his wife and his chauffeuse; The plight Kelly refers to here is the
single state he shared with Nicholson in their later years. He had up to this point lived either with his parents, briefly in digs in Kendal, in army
conditions or with Audrey and then Christine, so had rarely been alone; A blue plaque was placed on Nicholson's house soon after his death.*